A Purrrfect Time

Written by Sam Miller

Copyright © 2020 by Samuel Miller

All rights reserved. No part of this publication may be reproduced, stored in a retrieval system, or transmitted, in any form or by any means, electronic, mechanical, photocopying, recording, or otherwise, without the written prior permission of the publisher.

ISBN 978-1-7773038-0-8

Book design by Hiroki Nakaji

Armed Bandit Publishing

I met Sam when I was just a kitten. His life was easier then; he had both his arms. One day, Sam lost one of his arms in an accident, but he didn't lose his smile! This story is a reminder to focus on what makes you happy and to never give up. Join me as I look back at some moments from my life.

My name is Bob (the female cat) and I will tell this story.

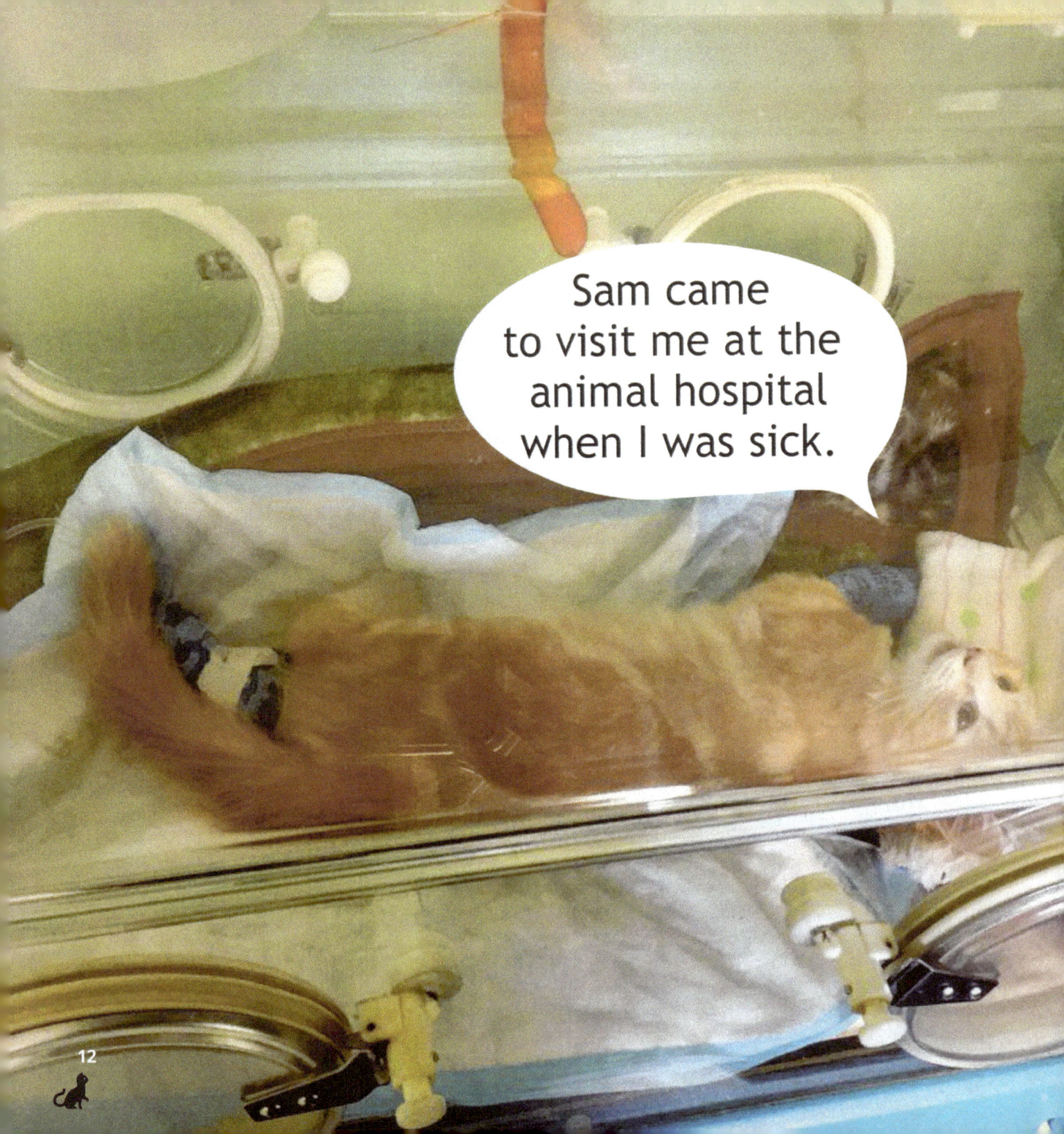

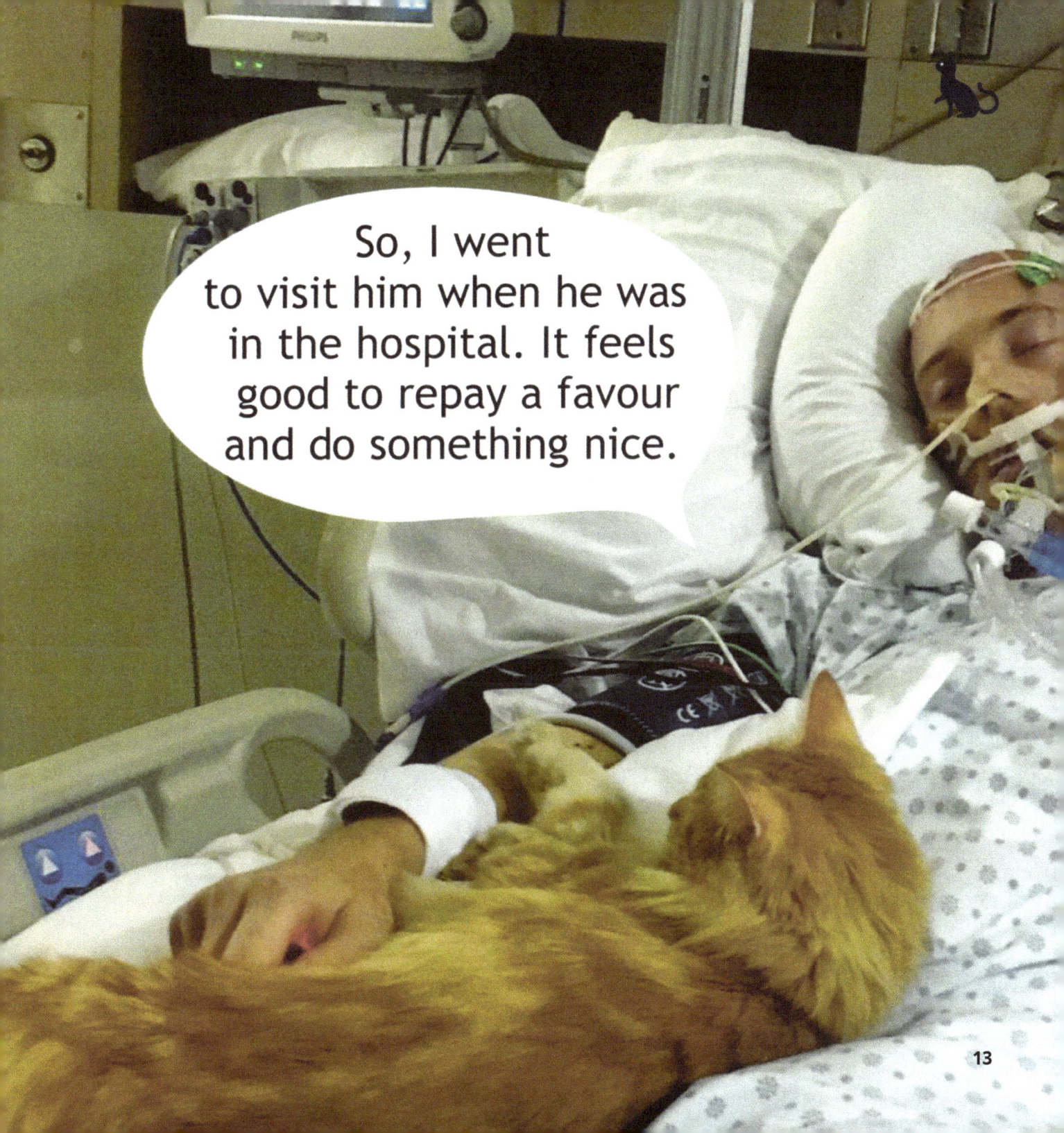

Sam was on the phone the other day and I heard him say this to his friend:

"Sometimes when I am talking to someone, I am not listening because I am thinking about what I am going to say. People want to be heard and know you are listening. I have realized it is very important to be focused on what they have to say to you, and then they will be interested in what you have to say to them.

"Who I am is reflected by the people I spend the most time with. I have made sure that I spend my time with people I trust, respect, and whose company I enjoy.

"When things are tough and I start to struggle or face a challenge, that's when I have found out a lot about myself and my friends. I have learned to embrace struggles and failures and reach out for help when needed."

Sam is right, I guess that is why he and I are such good friends!!

Did you find 🐈 on every picture page?

Sam: This book started out as a hobby for me. It was a way to distract me from the issues I was facing in my life. It turned out to be the therapy I needed. It taught me a lot about myself, as well as ways to deal with challenges and difficult situations.

For a long time, I thought I knew what life was all about and what mattered the most. I was very, very wrong. As I faced new challenges and overcame them, I started to realize what was important to me. I was then able to make an educated decision on what would really make me happy. There is no shame in failure and trying again. It is almost always the determined people who get what they want. You have to stay strong!

www.ingramcontent.com/pod-product-compliance
Lightning Source LLC
Chambersburg PA
CBHW051300110526
44589CB00025B/2896